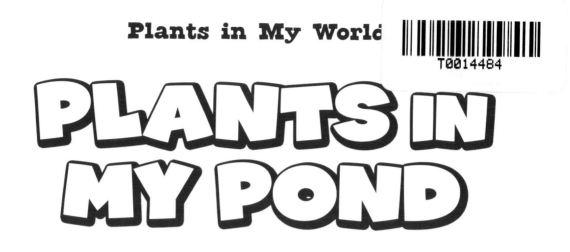

PLANTS IN MY POND

Porter Holmes

PowerKids
press.

NEW YORK

Published in 2018 by The Rosen Publishing Group, Inc.
29 East 21st Street, New York, NY 10010

First Edition

Editor: Theresa Morlock
Book Design: Michael Flynn

Photo Credits: Cover Humannet/Shutterstock.com; p. 5 Dimedrol68/Shutterstock.com; p. 6 Aleoks/Shutterstock.com; p. 9 E R DEGGINGER/Getty Images; p. 10 Judith Von Falkenhausen/EyeEm/Getty Images; p. 13 Shereena M/Shutterstock.com; p. 14 S.Z./Shutterstock.com; p. 17 Julie A Lynch/Shutterstock.com; p. 18 Vladimir Wrangel/Shutterstock/com; p. 21 lokvi/Shutterstock/com; p. 21 (inset) BMJ/Shutterstock/com; p. 22 Ricky John Molloy/Getty Images.

Cataloging-in-Publication Data

Names: Holmes, Porter.
Title: Plants in my pond / Porter Holmes.
Description: New York : PowerKids Press, 2018. | Series: Plants in my world | Includes index.
Identifiers: ISBN 9781538321249 (pbk.) | ISBN 9781538321263 (library bound) | ISBN 9781538321256 (6 pack)

Manufactured in China

CPSIA Compliance Information: Batch #BS17PK: For Further Information contact Rosen Publishing, New York, New York at 1-800-237-9932

Please visit: www.rosenpublishing.com and www.habausa.com

CONTENTS

Pond Plants

A pond is a small body of water surrounded by land. Ponds are homes to many kinds of animals and plants. What kinds of plants grow in ponds?

Cattails grow on the edge of a pond. They have a tall, thin stalk with a long narrow flower at the top. The wind blows away their fluffy white seeds.

Underwater

Hornwort plants grow at the bottom of a pond. Hornworts are also sometimes called coontails. That's because they look like the fluffy tail of a raccoon!

Floating Flowers

Water lilies float with their stems underwater. Their flowers can be pink, purple, blue, or white. Sometimes frogs rest on top of their smooth, wide leaves.

Water hyacinths creep across the top
of a pond. Their stems stick straight up.
Their beautiful flowers can be blue or purple.
Fish lay their eggs underneath the wide leaves.

Algae is a lot like a plant but isn't one. It's tiny and green with no leaves or a stem. Algae is good for a pond because it gives off oxygen, which animals need to breathe.

The plants and animals in a pond need each other. Plants give off oxygen. They also give animals food and homes. Plants need animals to spread their seeds.

Many Animals

What animals live in a pond? You might spot a turtle or a fish swimming by. Catfish are big and brown with long whiskers. Catfish eat water plants and water bugs.

Beavers make ponds when they build dams on streams. They have sharp front teeth, which they use to cut down trees and branches to build their homes.

Ponds are full of life. There are so many plants and animals to see! Ask your family if you can visit a pond. What other plants and animals will you see there?

WORDS TO KNOW

algae

cattail

dam

INDEX